Electric Wok Cookbook For Beginners

Simple Chinese Restaurant recipes and techniques for stir-frying, steaming, and Braising

Henrietta J. Rogge

This book is intended for informational purposes only and is not intended to test treat, cure, or prevent any disease. The reader should consult a medical professional before making any significant changes to their diet or lifestyle

Table of Content

Introduction

Years ago, I stumbled into a thriving Chinese restaurant supply store situated among the vibrant streets of Chinatown. I had a simple mission: find a bamboo steamer to experiment with homemade dumplings. Little did I realize that this expedition would lead me to a discovery that would permanently change my kitchen adventures

Among the rows of bamboo steamers and traditional cooking appliances, I noticed a shining work. It was unlike anything I'd seen before: it was made of solid carbon steel, had a round bottom, and exuded an authentic aura that whispered of sizzling stir-fries and fragrant steaming delicacies. It was just appealing.

Intrigued and probably impulsive, I decided to carry the wok home, picturing myself effortlessly stirring vegetables, meats, and sauces to create delectable dishes reminiscent of my favorite Chinese takeout dinners. Little did I know that this cheap purchase would set off an incredible culinary journey full of savory discoveries and delightful surprises.

As I began my electric wok cooking journey, I immediately realized that this multifunctional kitchen gadget was more than just a receptacle for stir-frying. It became my trusted companion, allowing me to experiment with a different range of cooking techniques, from steaming and braising to deep-frying, with ease and efficiency.

With each dish I made, I was enthralled by the unlimited possibilities that the electric wok provided. Whether I was making comfortable braised dishes, crispy fried treats, or experimenting with bold fusion flavors, the electric wok always delivered outstanding results.

Now, as I share my love of electric wok cooking with you through this cookbook, I welcome you to join me on a culinary journey unlike any other. Whether you're a professional chef or a curious beginner, this book will inspire and encourage you to unleash your culinary imagination, one delicious recipe at a time. So, dust off your electric wok, gather your supplies, and let us go on this wonderful journey together!

Why use an electric wok?

Welcome to the core of your electric wok journey! I know that at one point before you got this book, you might have asked, "Why choose an electric wok?" Okay, let's get started.

Versatility: An electric wok is like a multitasking magician in the kitchen. It does more than simply stir-fry; it also steams, braises, and deep-fries with finesse. From fast weeknight dishes to grandiose weekend feasts, your electric wok has you covered.

Ease of Use: Say goodbye to guessing and hello to clarity. Cooking with an electric wok is simple because it has precise temperature controls and equal heat distribution. Whether you're a beginner or an experienced cook, mastering the art of electric wok cooking is simple.

Space-Saving: Short on kitchen space? Not a problem! Unlike typical stovetop woks, electric woks are small and portable, making them ideal for small kitchens, dorm rooms, and even RVs. With an electric wok, you can prepare excellent dishes without cluttering your countertops.

Energy Efficiency: Let us discuss efficiency. Electric woks consume less energy than stovetop woks, allowing you to save big on utility bills while also lowering your carbon footprint. Cooking with an electric wok is also safer and less stressful because there are no open flames or gas leaks to worry about.

No-Fuss Cleanup: Nobody has time to clean burnt-on food! With its nonstick surface and dishwasher-safe pieces, washing up after cooking with an electric wok is a breeze. Simply wipe down or place in the dishwasher and you're ready to go.

In a nutshell, using an electric wok opens up a world of culinary options while minimizing the inconvenience. So, whether you want a classic stir-fry, a steaming bowl of dumplings, or a hearty braised dish, your electric wok is ready to cook everything - effortlessly, efficiently, and pleasantly.

Essential Tools & Ingredients

Before we enter into the delicious world of cooking, make sure you have all of the necessary tools and supplies.

Tools of the Trade: First and foremost, let's discuss the tools you'll need to release your inner chef with an electric wok. Of course, you'll need your trusty electric wok, but don't forget about additional necessities like a spatula for stirring, tongs for flipping, and a high-quality chef's knife for slicing up those fresh veggies. Oh, and don't forget the cutting board and measuring spoons - precision is essential in the kitchen!

Ingredients galore: Now, let's stock your pantry and refrigerator with all of the delicious ingredients that will elevate your electric wok dishes to the next level. From rich sauces and aromatic spices to crisp vegetables and sumptuous meats, there are many opportunities to discover. Don't be scared to be creative and experiment with new flavors and textures; that's what cooking is all about!

Fresh is Best: When it comes to ingredients, fresh is always preferred. So, head to your local farmers' market or the closest grocery store & stock up on the freshest produce, meats, and seafood you can find. Not only will your dishes taste better, but you'll also be supporting local farmers and businesses, which is a win-win!

Quality Counts: Remember that quality matters when it comes to ingredients. Choose organic whenever possible, and don't skimp on the good stuff. Whether it's a dab of high-quality soy sauce, a sprinkle of extra-virgin olive oil, or a sprinkling of fragrant herbs, employing high-quality ingredients will take your dishes from good to fantastic.

Stay Stocked: There's nothing worse than getting halfway through a meal and realizing you're missing an essential ingredient. Avoid cooking disasters by stocking your cupboard with the essentials, such as rice, noodles, oils, vinegars, and spices. This way, you'll always be prepared to cook a tasty supper at a moment's notice.

Armed with an electric wok and a well-stocked kitchen, you're ready to go on a culinary adventure full of flavor, inventiveness, and limitless possibilities. Roll up your sleeves, sharpen your knives, and let's start cooking!

Getting Acquainted With Your Electric Wok

Understanding Your Electric Wok.

Anatomy of an Electric Wok.

Let's get into the heart of your culinary arsenal: the electric wok. Consider it the Swiss Army knife for cooking; it is adaptable and ready for any culinary task. At its center is the cooking pan, which comes in round or flat-bottomed shapes and provides plenty of room for your culinary masterpieces. This pan is where the action takes place, whether you're stir-frying, steaming, or braising. The heating element, which drives the performance of your wok, is located beneath the pan. It heats rapidly and evenly, ensuring that your food cooks perfectly every time. Some electric woks even have changeable temperature controls, allowing you to precisely regulate the cooking process. And don't forget about the lid, which is a useful tool for sealing in flavors and moisture when steaming or boiling dishes. Understanding the structure of an electric wok is critical to maximizing its potential. So, educate yourself with its components and prepare to go on a culinary trip unlike any other!

Operating Your Electric Wok Safely

Now that you understand how your electric wok works let's go over how to use it securely. Safety should always be prioritized in the kitchen, and your electric wok is no different.

Step 1: Stable placement.

Before using your electric wok, make sure it is on a sturdy, flat surface away from combustible materials.

This helps prevent mishaps and keeps your wok secure while cooking.

Step 2: Temperature adjustment.

Familiarize yourself with the temperature controls on your electric wok.

Adjust the temperature to your recipe's specifications, but always begin with a lower setting & gradually increase as needed.

Step 3: Proper Handling

When using an electric wok, always use oven mitts or pot holders to safeguard your hands safe from heat.

To avoid burning or injuring yourself, never reach the heating element or hot surfaces directly.

Step 4: Attentive Cooking

Never leave an electric wok unattended while in use.

Stay vigilant and keep an eye on your cooking to avoid accidents and ensure everything runs properly.

Step 5: Cooling and Cleaning

Let your electric wok cool completely before cleaning it.

Clean the cooking surface with mild soap and water, but never immerse the entire machine in water to avoid electrical damage.

Following these safety precautions allows you to enjoy your electric wok cooking experience with confidence, knowing that you are protecting yourself and your kitchen from potential hazards.

Care and Maintenance Tips

Taking care of your electric wok guarantees that it will be a trustworthy kitchen partner for many years to come. Follow these basic care and maintenance steps to maintain your electric wok in good condition:

Clean after each use.

After cooking, let your electric wok cool completely before cleaning.

Ensure to clean the cooking surface with warm, soapy water & a gentle sponge or cloth, taking care not to scratch the nonstick coating.

Avoid abrasive cleaners.

Avoid using abrasive cleansers or scrubbers since they can damage your electric wok's nonstick surface.

Choose gentle detergents to protect the condition of your wok's surface.

Check Electrical Components.

Inspect the electrical cable and heating element on a regular basis for signs of wear and damage.

If you detect any problems, such as frayed cables or inconsistent heating, stop using it and contact an expert for repair.

Store properly.

When not in use, store your electric wok somewhere cool and dry.

Avoid putting/stacking heavy items on top of it since they can damage the cooking surface or heating element.

Regular maintenance

Perform frequent maintenance inspections to verify that your electric wok is working properly.

Remove any accumulated grease or food debris from the heating element to avoid impairing the wok's function.

By following these care & maintenance guidelines, you can extend the life of your electric wok and continue to cook great meals with ease.

Basic Techniques for Electric Wok Cooking

Stir-Frying Basics

Stir-frying is a versatile and popular cooking method commonly used in Asian cuisine. It involves quickly cooking small, uniform-sized pieces of food in a hot wok, making it a great fit for your electric wok. Here's how to use your electric wok for stir-frying like a pro:

Get Your Ingredients Ready

Make sure all of your ingredients are prepared & ready to use before you begin cooking. This includes slicing your meat or tofu, cleaning and chopping your veggies, and making any sauces or seasonings you plan to use.

Warm Up Your wok

Take a few minutes to heat up your electric wok on high heat so that it's nice and hot. A few drops of water added to the wok should sizzle and evaporate nearly instantly, indicating that it's ready.

Include Oil

When the wok is heated, coat the sides and bottom of the wok with a little quantity of oil by swirling it around. To keep oil from burning when cooking, use high smoke point oils like vegetable or peanut oil.

Begin to stir-fry

In the wok, add your ingredients in batches: add the aromatics (garlic, ginger, and onions), next the harder veggies (carrots, bell peppers), and lastly the softer ones (mushrooms, or leafy greens).

To ensure that the items cook evenly and don't stick to the bottom of the wok, mix and toss them frequently with a spatula.

Season and Serve

After the items are cooked to your desired consistency, add sauces, herbs, or spices to the stir-fry to suit your tastes.

As you serve your tasty stir-fry hot, savor the tastes and textures brought about by the high cooking temperature.

Gaining proficiency in the fundamentals of stir-frying with an electric wok will open up a world of culinary possibilities and make it simple for you to prepare tasty, quick dinners. Try varying the ingredients, sauces, and seasonings to create a unique and personalized version of stir-fries!

Steaming Essentials

Steaming Setup:

Make sure you have all the required essentials for steaming: an appropriate steaming rack or basket for your electric wok, a wok lid, and either parchment paper or cabbage leaves to avoid sticking.

Water Level:

Add water to the base of your electric wok, ensuring that it is below the steaming rack or basket. Be careful not to fill it too full to avoid boiling over while steaming.

Preheating:

Preheat the electric wok by adding water and bringing it to a gentle simmer or low boil. This will help generate steam quickly once the ingredients are added.

Ingredient Arrangement:

Arrange your ingredients on the steaming rack or basket in a single layer, making sure they are evenly spaced to allow for steam circulation. To ensure even cooking, avoid overcrowding.

Steaming Time:

The cooking duration differs depending on the thickness of the ingredients. Vegetables generally steam within 5-10 minutes, whereas proteins such as fish or chicken might require 10-20 minutes. To check if they are done, insert a fork or knife into the thickest part.

Flavor Enhancement:

Feel free to add herbs, spices, sauces, or aromatics such as ginger or garlic to impart flavor to your steamed dishes. Make sure to serve your dishes hot and savor the nutritious and delightful outcomes of using your electric wok for steaming!

Simple Braising Techniques

Braising involves using both dry and moist heat to produce tender and flavorful dishes. Your electric wok enables you to easily perfect this method for making a range of tasty meals.

Preparation:

Start by choosing your ingredients. Braising is effective with tougher meat cuts, like beef chuck or pork shoulder, and hearty vegetables, such as carrots, potatoes, and onions.

Searing:

Begin by browning the meat or vegetables in your electric wok. This process enhances the flavor and forms a caramelized outer layer. Use a modest quantity of oil and cook over high heat until all sides are browned.

Deglazing:

After searing the meat or vegetables, take them out of the wok and keep them aside. Pour some liquid into the wok, like broth, wine, or water, and use a spatula to scrape off any browned bits/remains from the bottom of the wok. This will enhance the flavor of the braising liquid.

Simmering:

Place the meat or vegetables back into the wok and let the liquid come to a gentle boil. Cover the wok with a lid and let the ingredients simmer over low heat to cook slowly. By cooking gently over low heat, the meat becomes tender, and the flavors blend together.

Seasoning:

Season the liquid used for braising with herbs, spices, and aromatics to suit your taste. Popular choices for flavorings include bay leaves, thyme, garlic, and onions.

Finishing:

After the meat has become tender and the vegetables have cooked through, take them out of the braising liquid and serve while hot. If desired, you can thicken the braising liquid to make a tasty sauce for the dish.

By using these straightforward braising methods, you can prepare comforting and fulfilling meals with your electric wok that will surely impress both family and friends.

Deep-Frying Made Easy

Deep-frying is a popular method of cooking that is famous for producing crispy and golden-brown treats. Using your electric wok, you can quickly and safely achieve perfect deep-frying results.

Deep-Frying Basics:

Preparation: Start by choosing your ingredients and getting them ready for deep-frying. This might involve covering meats, vegetables, or seafood in batter or breading to create a crunchy outer layer.

Oil Heating: Oil should be added to your electric wok, making sure it is deep enough to fully submerge the food. Choose an oil with a high smoke point, like vegetable or peanut oil, & heat it to the desired temperature using the wok's temperature control.

Frying Process: After the oil has reached the correct temperature, use tongs or a slotted spoon to carefully place the food into the wok. Be mindful not to overcrowd the wok, as this may cause the oil temp to decrease and lead to soggy food. If necessary, fry the food in batches to guarantee even cooking.

Cooking Time: Fry the food in hot oil until it turns golden brown & is fully cooked. The total time it takes to cook will depend on the type and size of the food being fried. Use a kitchen thermometer to make sure the inside reaches the right temperature for safe eating.

Draining and Serving: After cooking, use a slotted spoon or wire mesh skimmer to take the food out of the oil, and place it on a plate with the aid of a paper towel to drain off extra oil. Enjoy the hot and crispy deep-fried treats with your preferred dipping sauces or condiments.

By following these straightforward instructions, you can attain ideal deep-frying outcomes using your electric wok, enabling you to savor crunchy and delightful snacks from the convenience of your home kitchen.

Breakfast Recipes

Veggie Breakfast Stir-Fry

Ingredients:

- 2 eggs
- 1/2 bell pepper, thinly sliced
- 1/2 onion, thinly sliced
- 1 small tomato, diced
- 1 cup spinach leaves
- Salt and pepper to taste
- 1 tablespoon oil

Instructions:

1. Heat up the electric wok on medium-high heat.

2. Pour oil into the wok and stir-fry the bell pepper and onion until they are slightly softened.

3. Next, break the eggs into the wok and stir them until they are almost cooked.

4. Include diced tomato and spinach leaves, and stir until the spinach wilts.

5. Season with salt & pepper to your liking.

6. Serve while hot.

Serving Size: 2

Cooking Time: 10 minutes

Banana Pancakes

Ingredients:

- 1 ripe banana, mashed
- 1 egg
- 1/4 cup all-purpose flour
- 1/2 teaspoon baking powder
- Maple syrup or honey for serving
- Butter or oil for cooking

Instructions:

1. Mix together mashed banana and egg in a bowl until thoroughly combined.

2. Combine flour & baking powder, and stir until the mixture is smooth.

3. Begin by heating the electric wok over medium heat, then add a little quantity of butter or oil.

4. Pour about a quarter cup of pancake batter onto the wok for each pancake.

5. Next, you can cook the pancakes until bubbles start to form on the surface, then flip and continue cooking until both sides are golden brown.

6. Lastly, serve the pancakes while hot alongside maple syrup or honey.

Serving Size: 2

Cooking Time: 10 minutes

Breakfast Burrito Bowl

Ingredients:

- 2 eggs
- 1/2 cup cooked quinoa or rice
- 1/4 cup black beans that is drained and rinsed
- 1/4 cup diced tomatoes
- 1/4 cup diced avocado
- Salsa for serving
- Chopped cilantro for garnish
- Salt and pepper to taste
- 1 tablespoon oil

Instructions:

1. Begin by heating oil in the electric wok at medium heat.

2. Next, once the oil has become hot, crack/break the eggs into the wok & scramble them until they are fully cooked.

3. Next, combine the cooked quinoa or rice, black beans, and diced tomatoes in the wok, stirring until everything is heated through.

4. Season the mixture with salt & pepper according to your taste.

5. Finally, serve the prepared mixture in bowls and top it with diced avocado, salsa, and chopped cilantro.

Serving Size: 2

Cooking Time: 15 minutes

Coconut Milk Oatmeal

Ingredients:

- 1 cup rolled oats
- 1 1/2 cups coconut milk
- 1/2 cup water
- 1 tablespoon honey or maple syrup
- 1/4 teaspoon cinnamon
- Pinch of salt
- Fresh berries for serving
- Toasted coconut flakes for garnish

Instructions:

1.   Combine rolled oats, coconut milk, water, honey or maple syrup, cinnamon, and salt in the electric wok.

2.   Next, you can then cook the mixture over medium-low heat, stirring occasionally, until the oats are cooked and the mixture thickens, which should take about 10-15 minutes.

3.   When ready, serve the dish hot and top it with fresh berries & toasted coconut flakes.

Serving Size: 2

Cooking Time: 15 minutes

Spinach and Feta Omelette

Ingredients:

- 4 eggs
- 1/2 cup fresh spinach leaves
- 1/4 cup crumbled feta cheese
- Salt and pepper to taste
- 1 tablespoon oil

Instructions:

1. Beat/mix the eggs in a bowl until they are well mixed, and then season with salt and pepper.

2. Heat oil in an electric wok over medium heat.

3. Pour the beaten eggs into the wok, tilting to spread them evenly.

4. Sprinkle spinach leaves and feta cheese over one half of the omelette.

5. Lastly, fold the other half over the filling & cook until the eggs are set & the cheese is melted.

6. Serve the omelette hot.

Serving Size: 2

Cooking Time: 10 minutes

Apple Cinnamon French Toast

Ingredients:

- 4 slices bread
- 2 eggs
- 1/4 cup milk
- 1/2 teaspoon ground cinnamon
- 1/2 apple, thinly sliced
- Butter for cooking
- Maple syrup for serving

Instructions:

1. Whisk together eggs, milk, and ground cinnamon in a shallow dish.

2. Ensure that both sides of each bread slice are coated as you dip them into the egg mixture.

3. Heat butter in the electric wok over medium heat.

4. Cook the dipped bread slices in the wok until both sides are golden brown, which should take about 2-3 minutes per side.

5. Serve the cooked slices hot, topped with thinly sliced apples, and drizzled with maple syrup.

Serving Size: 2

Cooking Time: 10 minutes

Breakfast Quesadillas

Ingredients:

- 4 small flour tortillas
- 1/2 cup shredded cheese (you can use either of cheddar, mozzarella, or Mexican blend)
- 2 eggs, scrambled
- 1/4 cup diced bell peppers
- 1/4 cup diced onions
- Salsa and sour cream for serving
- Oil for cooking

Instructions:

1. Heat the oil in the electric wok on medium heat.

2. Place a tortilla in the wok and sprinkle it with shredded cheese.

3. On top of the cheese, add scrambled eggs, diced bell peppers, and diced onions.

4. Top it with another tortilla and gently press down.

5. Next, you can cook until the bottom tortilla has turned golden brown, then carefully flip it and cook the other side until golden brown and the cheese is melted.

6. Slice it into wedges & serve it hot, with salsa and sour cream on the side.

Serving Size: 2

Cooking Time: 10 minutes

Breakfast Hash

Ingredients:

- 2 potatoes, diced
- 1/4 cup diced onion
- 1/4 cup diced bell peppers
- 2 eggs
- Salt and pepper to taste
- 1 tablespoon oil
- Chopped parsley for garnish

Instructions:

1. Start by heating oil in the electric wok over medium-high heat.

2. Cook diced potatoes in the wok until they turn golden brown & crispy, stirring occasionally.

3. Add diced onion and bell peppers to the wok and keep cooking until they become softened.

4. Make two indentations in the hash and then crack an egg into each indentation.

5. Cover the wok and let the eggs cook until they have reached your preferred level of doneness.

6. Season with salt & pepper according to your taste & garnish with chopped parsley before serving.

Serving Size: 2

Cooking Time: 20 minutes

Teriyaki Chicken Stir-Fry

Ingredients:

- 2 boneless, skinless chicken breasts, sliced
- 1 cup broccoli florets
- 1/2 bell pepper, sliced
- 1/4 cup teriyaki sauce
- 2 tablespoons soy sauce
- 1 tablespoon sesame oil
- Cooked rice for serving

Instructions:

1. Preheat the electric wok on medium-high heat.

2. Sear the chicken in the wok with sesame oil until it's browned and fully cooked.

3. Once the chicken is done, add the broccoli florets and bell pepper slices, and cook until the vegetables are tender-crisp.

4. Drizzle the teriyaki sauce & soy sauce over the chicken and vegetables, and stir until everything is well coated and heated through.

5. Enjoy the dish hot with cooked rice.

Serving Size: 2

Cooking Time: 15 minutes

Vegetable Lo Mein

Ingredients:

- 8 oz (225g) lo mein noodles or you can use spaghetti
- 2 tablespoons vegetable oil
- 1 cup sliced mushrooms
- 1/2 cup julienned carrots
- 1/2 cup sliced bell peppers
- 2 cloves garlic, minced
- 1/4 cup soy sauce
- 1 tablespoon oyster sauce (optional)
- 1 teaspoon sesame oil
- Green onions for garnish

Instructions:

1. Fisrt thing is to cook the noodles while following the instructions on the package, then drain and set aside.

2. In the electric wok, heat vegetable oil over medium-high heat.

3. Stir-fry mushrooms, carrots, bell peppers, and garlic in the wok until the vegetables are tender.

4. Next, you can add the already cooked noodles to the wok, then toss with soy sauce, oyster sauce (if using), and sesame oil until well combined and heated through.

5. Lastly, garnish with chopped green onions and serve hot.

Serving Size: 2

Cooking Time: 15 minutes

Shrimp Fried Rice

Ingredients:

- 2 cups cooked rice, cooled
- 8 oz (225g) shrimp, peeled and deveined
- 1/2 cup frozen peas & carrots, thawed
- 2 eggs, beaten
- 2 tablespoons soy sauce
- 1 tablespoon oyster sauce
- 1 tablespoon sesame oil
- 2 green onions, chopped
- 2 cloves garlic, minced
- 1 tablespoon vegetable oil

Instructions:

1.   Heat the electric wok over medium heat and add vegetable oil.

2.   Stir the shrimp and garlic in the wok until the shrimp are pink & fully cooked, then set them aside.

3.   Scramble the beaten eggs in the wok until they are cooked, and then remove them from the wok and set them aside.

4.   Stir in the peas, carrots, soy sauce, oyster sauce, and sesame oil with the cooked rice in the wok, and stir-fry until heated through.

5.   Add the shrimp and eggs back into the wok and toss everything together until well combined.

6.   Garnish with chopped green onions & serve hot.

Serving Size: 2

Cooking Time: 20 minutes

Beef and Broccoli Stir-Fry

Ingredients:

- 8 oz (225g) beef sirloin, thinly sliced
- 1 cup broccoli florets
- 1/2 onion, sliced
- 2 cloves garlic, minced
- 1/4 cup soy sauce
- 1 tablespoon oyster sauce
- 1 tablespoon brown sugar
- 1 tablespoon cornstarch
- 1 tablespoon vegetable oil
- Cooked rice for serving

Instructions:

1. Combine soy sauce, oyster sauce, brown sugar, and cornstarch in a bowl to create the sauce. Keep it aside.

2. Heat vegetable oil in the electric wok on medium-high heat.

3. Cook beef slices in the wok, stirring constantly until they turn brown. Take them out of the wok and set aside.

4. Add broccoli florets, sliced onion, and minced garlic to the wok. Stir-fry until the vegetables are tender-crisp.

5. Put the beef back into the wok and pour the sauce over the mixture. Stir until everything is well coated & heated through.

6. Serve the dish hot over cooked rice.

Serving Size: 2

Cooking Time: 15 minutes

Thai Basil Chicken Stir-Fry

Ingredients:

- 2 boneless, skinless chicken breasts, sliced
- 1 bell pepper, sliced
- 1 onion, sliced
- 2 cloves garlic, minced
- 1/4 cup fresh basil leaves
- 2 tablespoons soy sauce
- 1 tablespoon oyster sauce
- 1 tablespoon fish sauce
- 1 tablespoon brown sugar
- 1 tablespoon vegetable oil

Instructions:

1. Heat up some vegetable oil in the electric wok over medium-high heat.

2. Cook the sliced chicken in the wok, stirring until it's cooked through. Take it out of the wok & set it aside.

3. In the same wok, stir-fry the sliced bell pepper, onion, and minced garlic until the vegetables are tender.

4. Put the cooked chicken back into the wok & add soy sauce, oyster sauce, fish sauce, and brown sugar. Stir until everything is well mixed & heated through.

5. Take the wok off the heat & stir in some fresh basil leaves.

6. Serve the dish hot over cooked rice.

Serving Size: 2

Cooking Time: 15 minutes

Lemon Garlic Shrimp Pasta

Ingredients:

- 8 oz (225g) spaghetti
- 8 oz (225g) shrimp, peeled and deveined
- 3 cloves garlic, minced
- Zest and juice of 1 lemon
- 2 tablespoons olive oil
- Salt and pepper to taste
- Chopped parsley for garnish

Instructions:

1. Cook the spaghetti while following the instructions on the package, then drain and set it aside.

2. Warm the olive oil in the electric wok over medium heat.

3. Sauté the minced garlic in the wok until it becomes fragrant.

4. Cook the shrimp in the wok until they turn pink and are fully cooked.

5. Mix in the lemon zest & juice, as well as salt and pepper.

6. Lastly, add the already cooked spaghetti to the wok & toss it until it's well coated.

7. Serve it hot, garnished with chopped parsley.

Serving Size: 2

Cooking Time: 15 minutes

Vegetable Tofu Stir-Fry

Ingredients:

- 8 oz (225g) firm tofu, cubed
- 1 cup mixed veggies (such as broccoli, bell peppers, carrots, and snow peas)
- 2 tablespoons soy sauce
- 1 tablespoon hoisin sauce
- 1 tablespoon rice vinegar
- 1 tablespoon sesame oil
- 2 cloves garlic, minced
- 1 tablespoon vegetable oil

Instructions:

1. Begin by heating vegetable oil in the electric wok over medium-high heat.

2. Stir-fry cubed tofu in the wok until it becomes golden brown on all sides, then remove it from the wok and set it aside.

3. In the same wok, stir-fry minced garlic and mixed vegetables until the vegetables are tender-crisp.

4. Add the cooked tofu back into the wok, then pour in soy sauce, hoisin sauce, rice vinegar, and sesame oil. Stir until everything is well coated & heated through.

5. Serve the dish hot over cooked rice.

Serving Size: 2

Cooking Time: 15 minutes

Dinner Recipes

Orange Ginger Beef Stir-Fry

Ingredients:

- 8 oz (225g) beef sirloin, thinly sliced
- 1 bell pepper, sliced
- 1 onion, sliced
- 2 cloves garlic, minced
- Zest and juice of 1 orange
- 2 tablespoons soy sauce
- 1 tablespoon hoisin sauce
- 1 tablespoon cornstarch
- 1 tablespoon vegetable oil

Instructions:

1.   In a mixing bowl, combine orange zest, orange juice, soy sauce, hoisin sauce, and cornstarch to create the sauce. Keep it aside.

2.   Warm up vegetable oil in the electric wok over medium-high heat.

3.   Cook the sliced beef in the wok, stirring until it browns. Take it out of the wok & set it aside.

4.   In the same wok, stir-fry the sliced bell pepper, onion, and minced garlic until the vegetables become tender.

5.   Put the cooked beef back in the wok and pour the sauce over the mixture. Stir until everything is thoroughly coated and heated through.

6.   Serve the dish hot over cooked rice.

Serving Size: 2

Cooking Time: 15 minutes

Lemon Garlic Chicken Pasta

Ingredients:

- 8 oz (225g) spaghetti
- 2 boneless, skinless chicken breasts, thinly sliced
- 3 cloves garlic, minced
- Zest and juice of 1 lemon
- 2 tablespoons olive oil
- Salt and pepper to taste
- Chopped parsley for garnish

Instructions:

1.   Spaghetti should be cooked as per the instructions on the package. After cooking, drain the spaghetti and set it aside.

2.   The electric wok should be heated over medium heat with olive oil.

3.   Minced garlic should be added to the wok and sautéed until fragrant.

4.   The sliced chicken should be added to the wok and cooked until browned and fully cooked.

5.   Lemon zest and juice, salt, and pepper should be stirred into the wok.

6.   The cooked spaghetti should be added to the wok and tossed until well coated.

7.   The dish should be served hot and garnished with chopped parsley.

Serving Size: 2

Cooking Time: 15 minutes

Spicy Peanut Tofu Stir-Fry

Ingredients:

- 8 oz (225g) firm tofu, cubed
- 1 bell pepper, sliced
- 1/2 onion, sliced
- 2 cloves garlic, minced
- 2 tablespoons soy sauce
- 2 tablespoons peanut butter
- 1 tablespoon sriracha sauce
- 1 tablespoon rice vinegar
- 1 tablespoon vegetable oil

Instructions:

1. Combine soy sauce, peanut butter, sriracha sauce, and rice vinegar in a bowl to create the sauce. Keep it aside.

2. Warm vegetable oil in the electric wok over medium-high heat.

3. Stir-fry cubed tofu in the wok until it turns golden brown on all sides. Take it out of the wok & set it aside.

4. In the same wok, stir-fry sliced bell pepper, onion, & minced garlic until the vegetables are tender-crisp.

5. Add the cooked tofu back to the wok and pour the sauce over the mixture. Stir until everything is well coated & heated through.

6. Serve the dish hot over cooked rice.

Serving Size: 2

Cooking Time: 15 minutes

Kung Pao Chicken

Ingredients:

- 2 boneless, skinless chicken breasts, diced
- 1/2 cup peanuts
- 1 bell pepper, diced
- 1/2 onion, diced
- 2 cloves garlic, minced
- 2 tablespoons soy sauce
- 1 tablespoon hoisin sauce
- 1 tablespoon rice vinegar
- 1 tablespoon cornstarch
- 1 tablespoon vegetable oil

Instructions:

1. Combine soy sauce, hoisin sauce, rice vinegar, and cornstarch in a bowl to create the sauce. Set aside.

2. Heat vegetable oil in an electric wok over medium-high heat.

3. Cook diced chicken in the wok, stirring until it browns and is fully cooked. Remove from the wok & set aside.

4. In the same wok, stir-fry peanuts, diced bell pepper, onion, and minced garlic until the vegetables are tender.

5. You can then return the cooked chicken to the wok and pour the sauce over the mixture. Stir until everything is well coated & heated through.

6. Serve the hot mixture over cooked rice.

Serving Size: 2

Cooking Time: 15 minutes

Garlic Sesame Shrimp Stir-Fry

Ingredients:

- 8 oz (225g) shrimp, peeled and deveined
- 2 cups mixed veggies (such as broccoli, bell peppers, & snap peas)
- 3 cloves garlic, minced
- 2 tablespoons soy sauce
- 1 tablespoon sesame oil
- 1 tablespoon honey
- 1 tablespoon vegetable oil

Instructions:

1. Heat up some vegetable oil in the electric wok over medium-high heat.

2. Sauté the minced garlic in the wok until it becomes fragrant.

3. Stir-fry the shrimp in the wok until they turn pink and are cooked through, then set them aside.

4. In the same wok, stir-fry the mixed vegetables until they are tender-crisp.

5. Add the cooked shrimp back in the wok and pour in soy sauce, sesame oil, and honey. Stir until everything is well coated & heated through.

6. Serve the dish hot over cooked rice.

Serving Size: 2

Cooking Time: 15 minutes

Vegetable Pad Thai

Ingredients:

- 8 oz (225g) rice noodles
- 1 cup mixed vegetables (such as bean sprouts, carrots, and green onions)
- 2 cloves garlic, minced
- 2 eggs, beaten
- 2 tablespoons soy sauce
- 1 tablespoon fish sauce
- 1 tablespoon tamarind paste
- 1 tablespoon brown sugar
- 1 tablespoon vegetable oil
- Crushed peanuts for garnish
- Lime wedges for serving

Instructions:

1.   First thing is to cook the rice noodles as per the directions/instructions on the pack, then drain them and set them aside.

2.   Heat some vegetable oil in the electric wok over medium-high heat.

3.   Sauté the minced garlic in the wok until it becomes fragrant.

4.   You can then push the garlic to one side of the wok & pour the already beaten eggs into the other side, then scramble them until they are fully cooked.

5.   Stir-fry the mixed vegetables in the wok until they become tender.

6.   Combine the cooked rice noodles, soy sauce, fish sauce, tamarind paste, and brown sugar in the wok, tossing everything until it is well mixed and heated through.

7.   Finally, serve the dish hot, garnished with crushed peanuts and lime wedges.

Serving Size: 2

Cooking Time: 15 minutes

Coconut Curry Chicken

Ingredients:

- 2 boneless, skinless chicken breasts, diced
- 1 bell pepper, diced
- 1/2 onion, diced
- 2 cloves garlic, minced
- 1 tablespoon curry powder
- 1 can (13.5 oz) coconut milk
- 1 tablespoon fish sauce
- 1 tablespoon vegetable oil
- Cooked rice for serving
- Chopped cilantro for garnish

Instructions:

1. Start by heating vegetable oil in the electric wok over medium-high heat.

2. Next, stir-fry the diced chicken in the wok until it's browned and cooked through, then set it aside.

3. In the same wok, stir-fry the diced bell pepper, onion, and minced garlic until the vegetables are tender.

4. Once the vegetables are tender, stir in the curry powder until it becomes fragrant.

5. After that, pour the coconut milk and fish sauce into the wok, stirring until everything is well combined.

6. Return the cooked chicken to the wok and let it simmer until it's heated through and the sauce thickens slightly.

7. Finally, serve the dish hot over, cooked rice and garnish it with chopped cilantro.

Serving Size: 2

Cooking Time: 20 minutes

Beef and Mushroom Chow Mein

Ingredients:

- 8 oz (225g) chow mein noodles
- 8 oz (225g) beef sirloin, thinly sliced
- 1 cup sliced mushrooms
- 1/2 bell pepper, sliced
- 1/2 onion, sliced
- 2 cloves garlic, minced
- 2 tablespoons soy sauce
- 1 tablespoon oyster sauce
- 1 tablespoon sesame oil
- 1 tablespoon vegetable oil

Instructions:

1. Cook the chow mein noodles as per the instructions on the package, then drain them and set them aside.

2. Heat some vegetable oil in the electric wok over medium-high heat.

3. Place the sliced beef in the wok and stir-fry until it browns. Then, remove it from the wok & set it aside.

4. In the same wok, add the sliced mushrooms, bell pepper, onion, and minced garlic. Stir-fry the veggies until they become tender.

5. Bring back the cooked beef to the wok & pour in the oyster sauce, soy sauce, & sesame oil. Stir until everything is well coated & heated through.

6. At this atge, you can then add the cooked chow mein noodles to the wok & toss until they are well combined.

7. Serve while hot.

Serving Size: 2

Cooking Time: 15 minutes

Poultry Recipes

Lemon Garlic Chicken Stir-Fry

Ingredients:

- 2 boneless, skinless chicken breasts, thinly sliced
- Zest and juice of 1 lemon
- 2 tablespoons soy sauce
- 2 cloves garlic, minced
- 1 tablespoon honey
- 1 tablespoon vegetable oil
- Salt and pepper to taste
- Chopped parsley for garnish

Instructions:

1. Combine lemon zest, lemon juice, soy sauce, minced garlic, honey, salt, & pepper in a bowl to create the marinade.

2. Marinate the sliced chicken in the mixture, ensuring it is well coated, and allow it to marinate for at least 15 minutes.

3. Warm vegetable oil in the electric wok over medium-high heat.

4. Stir-fry the marinated chicken in the wok until it is thoroughly cooked and has a light brown color.

5. Serve the dish hot, & garnish it with chopped parsley.

Serving Size: 2

Cooking Time: 15 minutes

Sesame Ginger Chicken Stir-Fry

Ingredients:

- 2 boneless, skinless chicken breasts, thinly sliced
- 2 tablespoons soy sauce
- 1 tablespoon sesame oil
- 1 tablespoon rice vinegar
- 1 tablespoon honey
- 2 cloves garlic, minced
- 1 tablespoon ginger, minced
- 1 tablespoon vegetable oil
- 1 tablespoon sesame seeds for garnish

Instructions:

1. Combine soy sauce, sesame oil, rice vinegar, honey, minced garlic, & minced ginger in a bowl to create the marinade.

2. Place the sliced chicken in the marinade, ensure it is coated, and allow it to marinate for at least 15 minutes.

3. Warm vegetable oil in the electric wok on medium-high heat.

4. You can then add the already marinated chicken to the wok and stir-fry until it is fully cooked and has a light brown color.

5. Serve the dish hot and sprinkle with sesame seeds for garnish.

Serving Size: 2

Cooking Time: 15 minutes

Spicy Szechuan Chicken

Ingredients:

- 2 boneless, skinless chicken breasts, diced
- 2 tablespoons soy sauce
- 1 tablespoon hoisin sauce
- 1 tablespoon rice vinegar
- 1 tablespoon chili garlic sauce
- 1 tablespoon vegetable oil
- 1/2 bell pepper, sliced
- 1/2 onion, sliced
- 2 cloves garlic, minced
- 1 tablespoon cornstarch combined with two tablespoons water

Instructions:

1. Mix together soy sauce, hoisin sauce, rice vinegar, and chili garlic sauce in a bowl to create the sauce.

2. On medium-high heat, heat vegetable oil in the electric wok.

3. Stir-fry diced chicken in the wok until it is browned and fully cooked.

4. Add sliced bell pepper, onion, and minced garlic to the wok and stir-fry until the vegetables are tender.

5. Pour the sauce over the chicken & vegetables in the wok and stir until everything is coated evenly.

6. Stir in the cornstarch-water mixture until the sauce thickens.

7. Serve the dish hot over cooked rice.

Serving Size: 2

Cooking Time: 15 minutes

Honey Garlic Chicken Wings

Ingredients:

- 1 lb (450g) chicken wings
- 3 tablespoons honey
- 2 tablespoons soy sauce
- 2 cloves garlic, minced
- 1 tablespoon vegetable oil
- Sesame seeds & sliced/chopped green onions for garnish

Instructions:

1. Combine honey, soy sauce, and minced garlic in a bowl to create the marinade.

2. You can then coat the chicken wings with the marinade & let them marinate for at least 30 minutes.

3. Heat vegetable oil in the electric wok over medium-high heat.

4. Cook the marinated chicken wings in the wok, turning occasionally, until they are golden brown & cooked through.

5. Garnish with sesame seeds & chopped green onions before serving hot.

Serving Size: 2

Cooking Time: 20 minutes

Coconut Curry Chicken

Ingredients:

- 2 boneless, skinless chicken breasts, diced
- 1 bell pepper, diced
- 1/2 onion, diced
- 2 cloves garlic, minced
- 1 tablespoon curry powder
- 1 can (13.5 oz) coconut milk
- 1 tablespoon fish sauce
- 1 tablespoon vegetable oil
- Cooked rice for serving
- Chopped cilantro for garnish

Instructions:

1. Begin by heating vegetable oil in the electric wok over medium-high heat.

2. Cook the diced chicken in the wok, stirring constantly until it is browned and fully cooked. Then, remove it from the wok & set it aside.

3. In the same wok, stir-fry the diced bell pepper, onion, and minced garlic until the vegetables are tender.

4. Sprinkle the vegetables with curry powder and stir until the aroma is released.

5. Combine the coconut milk and fish sauce in the wok, stirring thoroughly.

6. You can now add the cooked chicken back into the wok and let it simmer until heated through & the sauce thickens slightly.

7. Serve the dish hot over cooked rice, and garnish it with chopped cilantro.

Serving Size: 2

Cooking Time: 20 minutes

Teriyaki Chicken and Vegetable Skewers

Ingredients:

- 2 boneless, skinless chicken breasts that is cut into chunks
- 1 bell pepper, cut into chunks
- 1/2 onion, cut into chunks
- 1/2 cup teriyaki sauce
- Wooden skewers that is soaked in water for thirty minutes
- Sesame seeds for garnish

Instructions:

1.   Thread skewers with chicken, bell pepper, and onion.

2.   Electric wok should be preheated to medium-high heat.

3.   Apply teriyaki sauce on the skewers.

4.   Place skewers on the preheated wok & cook for eight to ten minutes, turning occasionally, until chicken is cooked through & veggies are tender.

5.   Garnish with sesame seeds and serve hot.

Serving Size: 2

Cooking Time: 15 minutes

Thai Basil Chicken Stir-Fry

Ingredients:

- 2 boneless, skinless chicken breasts, thinly sliced
- 1 bell pepper, sliced
- 1 onion, sliced
- 2 cloves garlic, minced
- 1/4 cup fresh basil leaves
- 2 tablespoons soy sauce
- 1 tablespoon oyster sauce
- 1 tablespoon fish sauce
- 1 tablespoon brown sugar
- 1 tablespoon vegetable oil

Instructions:

1. Heat up some vegetable oil in the electric wok over medium-high heat.

2. The sliced chicken should be added to the wok and stir-fried until cooked through, then removed and set aside.

3. In the same wok, stir-fry the sliced bell pepper, onion, and minced garlic until the vegetables are tender.

4. You can now return the cooked chicken to the wok & mix in soy sauce, oyster sauce, fish sauce, and brown sugar. Stir until everything is well coated & heated through.

5. Add fresh basil leaves to the wok & stir until they wilt.

6. Serve the dish hot over cooked rice.

Serving Size: 2

Cooking Time: 15 minutes

Lemon Herb Chicken Pasta

Ingredients:

- 8 oz (225g) spaghetti
- 2 boneless, skinless chicken breasts, thinly sliced
- Zest and juice of 1 lemon
- 2 cloves garlic, minced
- 2 tablespoons olive oil
- 1 tablespoon sliced fresh herbs (such as parsley, thyme, & rosemary)
- Salt and pepper to taste

Instructions:

1. Cook the spaghetti according to the instructions/directions on the package. After cooking, drain the spaghetti and set it aside.

2. Heat up some olive oil in the electric wok over medium heat.

3. Next, sauté the minced garlic in the wok until it becomes fragrant.

4. Then, add the sliced chicken to the wok and cook it until it turns brown and is fully cooked.

5. After that, stir in the lemon zest & juice, as well as the chopped fresh herbs, salt, and pepper.

6. Finally, add the cooked spaghetti to the wok and toss it until it is well coated. Serve the dish hot.

Serving Size: 2

Cooking Time: 15 minutes

Fish and Seafood Recipes

Garlic Butter Shrimp

Ingredients:

- 8 oz (225g) shrimp, peeled and deveined
- 2 tablespoons butter
- 3 cloves garlic, minced
- 1 tablespoon lemon juice
- Salt and pepper to taste
- Chopped parsley for garnish

Instructions:

1. Melt the butter in the electric wok over medium heat.
2. You can then sauté the minced garlic in the wok until fragrant.
3. Cook the shrimp in the wok until pink and opaque, about 2-3 minutes.
4. You can then mix in the lemon juice, salt, & pepper.
5. Serve the dish hot, topped with chopped parsley.

Serving Size: 2

Cooking Time: 5 minutes

Teriyaki Salmon

Ingredients:

- 2 salmon fillets
- 1/4 cup teriyaki sauce
- 1 tablespoon vegetable oil
- Sesame seeds for garnish
- Sliced green onions for garnish

Instructions:

1.   Marinate the salmon fillets in teriyaki sauce for 15-30 minutes.

2.   Warm vegetable oil in the electric wok over medium-high heat.

3.   Place the salmon fillets in the wok and cook for 4-5 minutes on each side or until they are cooked through.

4.   Serve while hot, and garnish with sesame seeds and sliced green onions.

Serving Size: 2

Cooking Time: 10 minutes

Thai Basil Shrimp Stir-Fry

Ingredients:

- 8 oz (225g) shrimp, peeled and deveined
- 1 bell pepper, sliced
- 1 onion, sliced
- 2 cloves garlic, minced
- 1/4 cup fresh basil leaves
- 2 tablespoons soy sauce
- 1 tablespoon oyster sauce
- 1 tablespoon fish sauce
- 1 tablespoon brown sugar
- 1 tablespoon vegetable oil

Instructions:

1. Heat up the electric wok over medium-high heat with vegetable oil.

2. Sauté the minced garlic in the wok until it becomes fragrant.

3. Stir-fry the shrimp in the wok until they turn pink and are fully cooked. Then, set them aside.

4. In the same wok, stir-fry the sliced bell pepper, onion, and fresh basil leaves until the vegetables become tender.

5. Return the cooked shrimp to the wok. Add soy sauce, oyster sauce, fish sauce, and brown sugar. Stir until everything is well-coated & heated through.

6. Serve the dish hot over cooked rice.

Serving Size: 2

Cooking Time: 15 minutes

Lemon Garlic Tilapia

Ingredients:

- 2 tilapia fillets
- 2 tablespoons butter
- 3 cloves garlic, minced
- Zest and juice of 1 lemon
- Salt and pepper to taste
- Chopped parsley for garnish

Instructions:

1. Melt butter in the electric wok over medium heat.

2. Sauté minced garlic in the wok until fragrant.

3. Cook tilapia fillets in the wok for 3-4 minutes on each side or until they are cooked through.

4. Add lemon zest and juice, salt, & pepper, and stir.

5. Serve garnished with chopped parsley while hot.

Serving Size: 2

Cooking Time: 10 minutes

Coconut Curry Shrimp

Ingredients:

- 8 oz (225g) shrimp, peeled and deveined
- 1 bell pepper, sliced
- 1/2 onion, sliced
- 2 cloves garlic, minced
- 1 tablespoon curry powder
- 1 can (13.5 oz) coconut milk
- 1 tablespoon fish sauce
- 1 tablespoon vegetable oil
- Cooked rice for serving
- Chopped cilantro for garnish

Instructions:

1. Begin by heating vegetable oil in the electric wok over medium-high heat.

2. Sauté the minced garlic in the wok until it becomes fragrant.

3. Stir-fry the shrimp in the wok until it turns pink and is cooked through. Then, remove it from the wok & set it aside.

4. In the same wok, stir-fry the sliced bell pepper, onion, and curry powder until the vegetables become tender.

5. Combine the coconut milk and fish sauce in the wok, stirring until well mixed.

6. Return the cooked shrimp to the wok and let it simmer until heated through and the sauce thickens slightly.

7. Serve the dish hot over cooked rice, garnished with chopped cilantro.

Serving Size: 2

Cooking Time: 15 minutes

Honey Garlic Glazed Salmon

Ingredients:

- 2 salmon fillets
- 3 tablespoons honey
- 2 tablespoons soy sauce
- 2 cloves garlic, minced
- 1 tablespoon rice vinegar
- 1 tablespoon vegetable oil
- Sesame seeds for garnish
- Sliced green onions for garnish

Instructions:

1. Combine honey, soy sauce, minced garlic, and rice vinegar in a bowl to create the glaze.

2. Warm vegetable oil in the electric wok on medium-high heat.

3. Cook salmon fillets in the wok for 3-4 minutes on each side or until they are fully cooked.

4. Apply the honey garlic glaze to the salmon while cooking.

5. Serve the dish hot, topped with sesame seeds and sliced green onions.

Serving Size: 2

Cooking Time: 10 minutes

Spicy Stir-Fried Squid

Ingredients:

- 8 oz (225g) squid, cleaned and sliced
- 1 bell pepper, sliced
- 1/2 onion, sliced
- 2 cloves garlic, minced
- 1 tablespoon soy sauce
- 1 tablespoon oyster sauce
- 1 tablespoon chili garlic sauce
- 1 tablespoon vegetable oil
- Chopped green onions for garnish

Instructions:

1. Heat the electric wok over medium-high heat and add vegetable oil.

2. Sauté the minced garlic in the wok until it becomes fragrant.

3. Stir-fry the sliced squid in the wok for 2-3 minutes.

4. Add soy sauce, oyster sauce, and chili garlic sauce, along with the sliced bell pepper and onion, & stir-fry until the vegetables are tender and the squid is cooked through.

5. Garnish with chopped green onions & serve hot.

Serving Size: 2

Cooking Time: 10 minutes

Thai Green Curry Shrimp

Ingredients:

- 8 oz (225g) shrimp, peeled and deveined
- 1 bell pepper, sliced
- 1/2 onion, sliced
- 2 tablespoons Thai green curry paste
- 1 can (13.5 oz) coconut milk
- 1 tablespoon fish sauce
- 1 tablespoon vegetable oil
- Cooked rice for serving
- Fresh cilantro for garnish

Instructions:

1. Heat up some vegetable oil in the electric wok on medium-high heat.

2. Sauté the Thai green curry paste in the wok until it becomes fragrant.

3. Stir-fry the shrimp in the wok until they turn pink and are cooked through. Then, set them aside.

4. In the same wok, stir-fry the sliced bell pepper and onion until the vegetables become tender.

5. Combine the coconut milk and fish sauce in the wok, stirring well.

6. Add the cooked shrimp back to the wok and simmer until heated through and the sauce thickens slightly.

7. Serve the dish hot over cooked rice, and garnish it with fresh cilantro.

Serving Size: 2

Cooking Time: 15 minutes

Vegetarian Recipes

Vegetable Stir-Fry

Ingredients:

- 2 cups mixed veggies (bell peppers, broccoli, carrots, & snap peas), sliced
- 2 cloves garlic, minced
- 2 tablespoons soy sauce
- 1 tablespoon sesame oil
- 1 tablespoon vegetable oil
- Salt and pepper to taste
- Cooked rice or noodles for serving

Instructions:

1. Heat up some vegetable oil in the electric wok on medium-high heat.
2. Sauté the minced garlic in the wok until it becomes fragrant.
3. Stir-fry the mixed vegetables in the wok until they are tender-crisp.
4. Mix in soy sauce & sesame oil, and season with salt and pepper to taste.
5. Lastly, serve the stir-fry hot over cooked rice or noodles.

Serving Size: 2

Cooking Time: 10 minutes

Tofu and Vegetable Teriyaki Stir-Fry

Ingredients:

- 1 block firm tofu, cubed
- 2 cups mixed vegetables (such as bell peppers, broccoli, and mushrooms), sliced
- 2 cloves garlic, minced
- 1/4 cup teriyaki sauce
- 1 tablespoon vegetable oil
- Cooked rice for serving
- Sesame seeds for garnish

Instructions:

1. Heat the electric wok over medium-high heat and add vegetable oil.

2. Cook cubed tofu in the wok until it turns golden brown on all sides. Then, set it aside.

3. Sauté minced garlic in the wok until it becomes fragrant.

4. Stir-fry mixed vegetables in the wok until they become tender.

5. Put the cooked tofu back into the wok and pour teriyaki sauce over the tofu and vegetables. Stir until everything is well coated & heated through.

6. Serve the dish hot over cooked rice, and garnish with sesame seeds.

Serving Size: 2

Cooking Time: 15 minutes

Eggplant and Tofu Stir-Fry

Ingredients:

- 1 small eggplant, cubed
- 1 block firm tofu, cubed
- 2 cloves garlic, minced
- 2 tablespoons soy sauce
- 1 tablespoon hoisin sauce
- 1 tablespoon vegetable oil
- Cooked rice for serving
- Chopped cilantro for garnish

Instructions:

1. Heat up the vegetable oil in the electric wok on a medium-high setting.

2. Toss the cubed eggplant into the wok and stir-fry until it becomes tender.

3. Sauté the minced garlic in the wok until it becomes fragrant.

4. Stir-fry the cubed tofu in the wok until it turns golden brown.

5. Mix in the soy sauce and hoisin sauce, ensuring everything is well coated and heated through.

6. Serve the dish hot over cooked rice, and garnish with chopped cilantro.

Serving Size: 2

Cooking Time: 15 minutes

Vegetable Curry

Ingredients:

- 2 cups mixed veggies (such as potatoes, carrots, peas, & bell peppers), diced
- 1 onion, diced
- 2 cloves garlic, minced
- 1 can (13.5 oz) coconut milk
- 2 tablespoons curry powder
- 1 tablespoon vegetable oil
- Cooked rice for serving
- Chopped cilantro for garnish

Instructions:

1. Begin by heating vegetable oil in the electric wok over medium-high heat.
2. Sauté diced onion in the wok until it becomes translucent.
3. Sauté minced garlic in the wok until it becomes fragrant.
4. Add mixed vegetables to the wok and stir-fry until they are slightly softened.
5. Stir in curry powder over the vegetables until it becomes fragrant.
6. Combine coconut milk into the wok and stir thoroughly.
7. Let it simmer until the vegetables are tender and the sauce thickens slightly.
8. Serve the dish hot over cooked rice, and garnish with chopped cilantro.

Serving Size: 2

Cooking Time: 20 minutes

Vegetarian Pad Thai

Ingredients:

- 8 oz (225g) rice noodles
- 1 cup mixed vegetables (such as bean sprouts, carrots, and green onions)
- 2 cloves garlic, minced
- 2 eggs, beaten
- 2 tablespoons soy sauce
- 1 tablespoon fish sauce
- 1 tablespoon tamarind paste
- 1 tablespoon brown sugar
- 1 tablespoon vegetable oil
- Crushed peanuts for garnish
- Lime wedges for serving

Instructions:

1. Cook the rice noodles while following the instructions on the package, then drain them & set them aside.
2. In the electric wok, heat the vegetable oil over medium-high heat.
3. Sauté the minced garlic in the wok until it becomes fragrant.
4. Move the garlic to one side of the wok & then you can pour the beaten eggs into the other side.
5. You can then scramble the eggs until they are cooked through.
6. Next, add the mixed veggies to the wok and stir-fry them until they are tender.
7. Mix in the cooked rice noodles, soy sauce, fish sauce, tamarind paste, and brown sugar. Toss everything together until it is well combined and heated through.
8. Serve the dish hot, garnished with crushed peanuts and lime wedges.

Serving Size: 2

Cooking Time: 15 minutes

Vegetable Fried Rice

Ingredients:

- 2 cups cooked rice
- 2 cups mixed veggies (carrots, corn, & green beans)
- 2 cloves garlic, minced
- 2 eggs, beaten
- 2 tablespoons soy sauce
- 1 tablespoon sesame oil
- 1 tablespoon vegetable oil
- Sliced green onions for garnish

Instructions:

1. Heat up the electric wok with vegetable oil over medium-high heat.
2. Sauté the minced garlic in the wok until it becomes fragrant.
3. Move the garlic to one side of the wok & pour the beaten eggs into the empty space. You can then scramble the eggs until they are fully cooked.
4. Stir-fry the mixed vegetables in the wok until they become tender.
5. Combine the cooked rice, soy sauce, and sesame oil in the wok. Toss all the mixture together until it is well mixed & heated through.
6. Lastly, serve the dish hot, and garnish it with sliced green onions.

Serving Size: 2

Cooking Time: 10 minutes

Sweet and Sour Tofu

Ingredients:

- 1 block firm tofu, cubed
- 1 bell pepper, diced
- 1/2 onion, diced
- 1 cup pineapple chunks
- 1/4 cup sweet and sour sauce
- 1 tablespoon vegetable oil
- Cooked rice for serving

Instructions:

1.   Heat up the vegetable oil in the electric wok on medium-high heat.

2.   Cook the cubed tofu in the wok until it turns golden brown on all sides. Then, bring it out & keep it aside.

3.   Stir-fry the diced bell pepper and onion in the wok until they become tender.

4.   Put the cooked tofu back in the wok, then add pineapple chunks and sweet and sour sauce. Stir until everything is well coated & heated through.

5.   Serve the dish hot on top of cooked rice.

Serving Size: 2

Cooking Time: 15 minutes

Beef and Pork Recipes

Pork and Vegetable Stir-Fry

Ingredients:

- 8 oz (225g) pork loin, thinly sliced
- 2 cups mixed veggies (bell peppers, snow peas, & carrots), sliced
- 2 cloves garlic, minced
- 2 tablespoons soy sauce
- 1 tablespoon hoisin sauce
- 1 tablespoon vegetable oil
- Cooked rice for serving
- Sliced green onions for garnish

Instructions:

1. Begin by heating vegetable oil in the electric wok over a medium-high heat.

2. Sauté the minced garlic in the wok until it becomes fragrant.

3. Stir-fry the thinly sliced pork loin in the wok until it browns.

4. Stir-fry the mixed vegetables in the wok until they become tender.

5. Combine soy sauce and hoisin sauce into the wok and toss until everything is well coated and heated through.

6. Serve the dish hot over cooked rice, and garnish with sliced green onions.

Serving Size: 2

Cooking Time: 10 minutes

Mongolian Beef

Ingredients:

- 8 oz (225g) beef flank steak, thinly sliced
- 2 tablespoons cornstarch
- 2 tablespoons vegetable oil
- 2 cloves garlic, minced
- 1/4 cup soy sauce
- 1/4 cup brown sugar
- 2 green onions, sliced
- Cooked rice for serving
- Sesame seeds for garnish

Instructions:

1. Coat thinly sliced beef flank steak with cornstarch, ensuring even coverage.
2. In an electric wok set to medium-high heat, heat vegetable oil.
3. Sauté minced garlic in the wok until it becomes fragrant.
4. Next, add the beef to the wok & stir-fry until it browns.
5. Mix in soy sauce and brown sugar, cooking until the sauce slightly thickens.
6. Top with sliced green onions & sesame seeds for garnish.
7. Serve the dish hot over cooked rice.

Serving Size: 2

Cooking Time: 15 minutes

Kung Pao Pork

Ingredients:

- 8 oz (225g) pork tenderloin, diced
- 1/2 cup peanuts
- 2 tablespoons vegetable oil
- 2 cloves garlic, minced
- 2 tablespoons soy sauce
- 1 tablespoon hoisin sauce
- 1 tablespoon rice vinegar
- 1 tablespoon brown sugar
- Cooked rice for serving

Instructions:

1. Heat up the vegetable oil in the electric wok on medium-high heat.

2. Introduce the diced pork tenderloin to the wok and stir-fry until it turns brown.

3. Sauté the minced garlic in the wok until it becomes fragrant.

4. Mix in the soy sauce, hoisin sauce, rice vinegar, and brown sugar.

5. Toss the peanuts into the wok and ensure everything is well coated and heated through.

6. Serve the dish hot over cooked rice.

Serving Size: 2

Cooking Time: 15 minutes

Pork Fried Rice

Ingredients:

- 2 cups cooked rice
- 8 oz (225g) pork loin, diced
- 1 cup mixed veggies (peas, carrots, & corn)
- 2 cloves garlic, minced
- 2 eggs, beaten
- 2 tablespoons soy sauce
- 1 tablespoon vegetable oil
- Sliced green onions for garnish

Instructions:

1. Start by heating vegetable oil in the electric wok over medium-high heat.

2. Sauté minced garlic in the wok until it becomes fragrant.

3. After sautéing the garlic, move it to one side of the wok and pour the beaten eggs into the other side. You can then scramble the eggs until they are fully cooked.

4. Stir-fry diced pork loin in the wok until it is browned.

5. Stir-fry the mixed vegetables in the wok until they are tender.

6. Combine the cooked rice and soy sauce with the stir-fried ingredients in the wok. Toss everything together until it is well combined and heated through.

7. Serve the dish hot, garnished with sliced green onions.

Serving Size: 2

Cooking Time: 10 minutes

Beef and Mushroom Stir-Fry

Ingredients:

- 8 oz (225g) beef sirloin, thinly sliced
- 2 cups mushrooms, sliced
- 2 cloves garlic, minced
- 2 tablespoons soy sauce
- 1 tablespoon oyster sauce
- 1 tablespoon vegetable oil
- Cooked rice for serving

Instructions:

1. Heat the electric wok over medium-high heat and add vegetable oil.

2. Sauté minced garlic in the wok until it becomes fragrant.

3. Stir-fry thinly sliced beef in the wok until it browns.

4. Stir-fry sliced mushrooms in the wok until they become tender.

5. Combine soy sauce and oyster sauce into the wok, tossing until everything is well coated and heated through.

6. Lastly, serve the stir-fry hot over, cooked rice.

Serving Size: 2

Cooking Time: 10 minutes

Sweet and Sour Pork

Ingredients:

- 8 oz (225g) pork tenderloin, diced
- 1 bell pepper, diced
- 1/2 onion, diced
- 1 cup pineapple chunks
- 1/4 cup sweet and sour sauce
- 1 tablespoon vegetable oil
- Cooked rice for serving

Instructions:

1. Heat up the vegetable oil in the electric wok on medium-high heat.

2. Once the oil is hot, stir-fry the diced pork tenderloin in the wok until it is browned.

3. Next, stir-fry the diced bell pepper and onion in the wok until they are tender.

4. After that, add the pineapple chunks and sweet and sour sauce to the wok. Toss all the mixture together until it is well coated & heated through.

5. Finally, serve the dish hot over cooked rice.

Serving Size: 2

Cooking Time: 15 minutes

Pork and Ginger Stir-Fry

Ingredients:

- 8 oz (225g) pork loin, thinly sliced
- 2 tablespoons soy sauce
- 1 tablespoon oyster sauce
- 1 tablespoon rice vinegar
- 1 tablespoon vegetable oil
- 1 tablespoon fresh ginger, minced
- Cooked rice for serving
- Sliced green onions for garnish

Instructions:

1. Mix soy sauce, oyster sauce, and rice vinegar in a bowl. Keep aside.
2. Electric wok should be heated over medium-high heat with vegetable oil.
3. Sauté minced ginger in the wok until fragrant.
4. Stir-fry thinly sliced pork loin in the wok until browned.
5. Toss the pork with the sauce mixture until well coated and heated through.
6. Serve the dish hot over cooked rice, and garnish with sliced green onions.

Serving Size: 2

Cooking Time: 10 minutes

Soup Recipes

Hot and Sour Soup

Ingredients:

- 4 cups vegetable broth
- 1/2 cup tofu, diced
- 1/4 cup bamboo shoots, sliced
- 1/4 cup mushrooms, sliced
- 2 tablespoons soy sauce
- 2 tablespoons rice vinegar
- 1 tablespoon chili paste
- 1 tablespoon cornstarch (combined with two tablespoons water)
- 1 egg, beaten
- Sliced green onions for garnish

Instructions:

1.   Heat vegetable broth until it simmers over medium heat in the wok

2.   Toss in diced tofu, sliced bamboo shoots, and sliced mushrooms. Let it cook for 5 minutes.

3.   Mix in soy sauce, rice vinegar, and chili paste. Let it simmer for more five(5) minutes.

4.   While stirring continuously, slowly pour the beaten egg into the soup to create egg ribbons.

5.   Thicken the soup by stirring in the cornstarch mixture.

6.   Lastly, garnish with sliced green onions & serve hot.

Serving Size: 4

Cooking Time: 15 minutes

Miso Soup

Ingredients:

- 4 cups vegetable broth
- 1/4 cup miso paste
- 1/2 cup tofu, diced
- 1/4 cup seaweed, sliced
- Sliced green onions for garnish

Instructions:

1. Heat vegetable broth in the electric wok over medium heat until it simmers.
2. Mix miso paste in a small bowl with a little hot broth until it forms a smooth paste.
3. Stir in the miso paste to the wok until it is well combined.
4. Add diced tofu and sliced seaweed to the wok and let it simmer for 5 minutes.
5. Serve hot with sliced green onions as a garnish.

Serving Size: 4

Cooking Time: 10 minutes

Tom Yum Soup

Ingredients:

- 4 cups vegetable broth
- 1 stalk lemongrass, smashed
- 3 slices galangal (Thai ginger)
- 3 kaffir lime leaves
- 2 tablespoons soy sauce
- 1 tablespoon chili paste
- 1/4 cup mushrooms, sliced
- 1/4 cup cherry tomatoes, halved
- 1/4 cup tofu, diced
- 1 tablespoon lime juice
- Sliced green onions for garnish
- Chopped cilantro for garnish

Instructions:

1. Heat vegetable broth in the electric wok over medium-high heat until it boils.

2. Add crushed lemongrass, slices of galangal, and kaffir lime leaves to the wok, and let it simmer for 5 minutes.

3. Mix in soy sauce and chili paste.

4. Introduce sliced mushrooms, halved cherry tomatoes, and diced tofu to the wok and let it simmer for another 5 minutes.

5. Stir in lime juice.

6. When serving, garnish with sliced green onions and chopped cilantro.

Serving Size: 4

Cooking Time: 15 minutes

Vegetable Noodle Soup

Ingredients:

- 4 cups vegetable broth
- 2 oz (60g) rice noodles
- 1 cup mixed veggies (carrots, bell peppers, & snow peas), sliced
- 2 tablespoons soy sauce
- 1 tablespoon sesame oil
- Sliced green onions for garnish

Instructions:

1. Heat vegetable broth in the electric wok over medium-high heat until it boils.

2. Cook the rice noodles in the wok following the instructions on the package.

3. Simmer sliced mixed vegetables, soy sauce, and sesame oil until the vegetables are tender.

4. Lastly, garnish with sliced green onions & serve hot.

Serving Size: 4

Cooking Time: 10 minutes

Thai Coconut Soup

Ingredients:

- 4 cups vegetable broth
- 1 can (13.5 oz) coconut milk
- 1 stalk lemongrass, smashed
- 3 slices galangal (Thai ginger)
- 3 kaffir lime leaves
- 1 tablespoon soy sauce
- 1 tablespoon lime juice
- 1/4 cup mushrooms, sliced
- 1/4 cup cherry tomatoes, halved
- Sliced green onions for garnish
- Chopped cilantro for garnish

Instructions:

1.   In a electric wok, heat vegetable broth over medium-high heat until it boils.

2.   Combine coconut milk, crushed lemongrass, galangal slices, and kaffir lime leaves in the wok. Let it simmer for more five(5) minutes.

3.   Mix in soy sauce and lime juice.

4.   Place sliced mushrooms and halved cherry tomatoes in the wok. Let it simmer for additional five(5) minutes.

5.   Serve the dish hot, topped with sliced green onions and chopped cilantro.

Serving Size: 4

Cooking Time: 15 minutes

Spicy Szechuan Soup

Ingredients:

- 4 cups vegetable broth
- 2 tablespoons Szechuan peppercorns
- 2 tablespoons chili oil
- 2 tablespoons soy sauce
- 1 tablespoon rice vinegar
- 1/4 cup tofu, diced
- 1/4 cup bamboo shoots, sliced
- Sliced green onions for garnish

Instructions:

1.   Bring the veggie broth to a boil over medium-high heat in the electric wok.

2.   The wok should have Szechuan peppercorns, chili oil, soy sauce, and rice vinegar added to it. Let it simmer for 5 minutes.

3.   After that, stir in diced tofu and sliced bamboo shoots and let it simmer for another 5 minutes.

4.   Lastly, garnish with sliced green onions & serve hot.

Serving Size: 4

Cooking Time: 10 minutes

Lentil and Vegetable Soup

Ingredients:

- 4 cups vegetable broth
- 1 cup lentils
- 1 cup mixed vegetables (such as carrots, celery, and potatoes), diced
- 2 cloves garlic, minced
- 1 teaspoon cumin
- 1 teaspoon paprika
- Salt and pepper to taste
- Chopped parsley for garnish

Instructions:

1. Heat vegetable broth in the electric wok over medium-high heat until boiling.

2. Combine lentils, mixed vegetables, minced garlic, cumin, and paprika in the wok. Let it simmer until the lentils & vegetables are tender.

3. Add salt and pepper to taste.

4. Garnish with chopped parsley and serve hot.

Serving Size: 4

Cooking Time: 20 minutes

Corn and Potato Chowder

Ingredients:

- 4 cups vegetable broth
- 2 cups corn kernels
- 2 potatoes, diced
- 1 onion, diced
- 2 cloves garlic, minced
- 1/2 cup coconut milk
- Salt and pepper to taste
- Chopped chives for garnish

Instructions:

1.   Start by first bringing the veggie broth to a boil over medium-high heat in the electric wok.

2.   The wok should have corn kernels, diced potatoes, diced onion, and minced garlic added to it, and then simmer until the potatoes are tender.

3.   After that, stir in coconut milk and let it simmer for another 5 minutes.

4.   Finally, season with salt & pepper to taste & serve hot, garnished with chopped chives.

Serving Size: 4

Cooking Time: 20 minutes

Salad and Sauces Recipes

Asian Sesame Salad Dressing

Ingredients:

- 1/4 cup soy sauce
- 2 tablespoons rice vinegar
- 1 tablespoon sesame oil
- 1 tablespoon honey
- 1 clove garlic, minced
- 1 teaspoon grated ginger
- 1 tablespoon sesame seeds

Instructions:

1.   Combine/Mix soy sauce, rice vinegar, sesame oil, honey, minced garlic, and grated ginger in the electric wok.

2.   You can then stir frequently over low heat until the mixture is well combined and heated through.

3.   Once heated, remove the wok from the heat and mix in the sesame seeds.

4.   Next, allow the dressing to cool down before using it.

5.   Drizzle over your preferred salad greens when serving.

Serving Size: Makes about 1/2 cup

Cooking Time: 5 minutes

Sweet Chili Sauce

Ingredients:

- 1/2 cup rice vinegar
- 1/2 cup water
- 1/2 cup granulated sugar
- 2 tablespoons soy sauce
- 1 tablespoon cornstarch
- 1 tablespoon water
- 2 cloves garlic, minced
- 1 teaspoon grated ginger
- 2 red chili peppers, finely chopped (seeds removed for less heat)

Instructions:

1. Combine rice vinegar, water, sugar, soy sauce, minced garlic, grated ginger, and chopped red chili peppers in the electric wok.

2. Next, warm the mixture over medium heat until it starts to simmer.

3. Create a slurry by mixing/combining cornstarch with water in a small bowl.

4. Thicken the sauce by stirring the cornstarch slurry into it and cooking while stirring constantly.

5. Allow the sauce to cool before using.

6. Lastly, serve the sauce as a dipping sauce or drizzle it over grilled meats or vegetables.

Serving Size: Makes about 1 cup

Cooking Time: 10 minutes

Spicy Peanut Sauce

Ingredients:

- 1/2 cup peanut butter
- 1/4 cup soy sauce
- 2 tablespoons rice vinegar
- 2 tablespoons honey
- 1 clove garlic, minced
- 1 teaspoon grated ginger
- 1 tablespoon sriracha sauce (adjust to taste)
- 2 tablespoons water (optional for thinning)

Instructions:

1.   Combine peanut butter, soy sauce, rice vinegar, honey, minced garlic, grated ginger, and sriracha sauce in the electric wok.

2.   Keep stirring frequently over low heat until the mixture is well combined.

3.   If you observe that the sauce is too thick, you can add some water to reach the desired consistency.

4.   Allow the sauce to cool before serving.

5.   Lastly, use it as a dipping sauce for spring rolls or drizzle it over noodles or salads.

Serving Size: Makes about 1 cup

Cooking Time: 5 minutes

Thai Peanut Salad Dressing

Ingredients:

- 1/4 cup peanut butter
- 2 tablespoons soy sauce
- 2 tablespoons lime juice
- 1 tablespoon honey
- 1 clove garlic, minced
- 1 teaspoon grated ginger
- 2 tablespoons water (optional for thinning)

Instructions:

1. Combine peanut butter, soy sauce, lime juice, honey, minced garlic, and grated ginger in the electric wok.

2. Keep stirring constantly over low heat until the mixture is well combined.

3. If the dressing is too thick, add water to reach the desired consistency.

4. Allow the dressing to cool before serving.

5. Lastly, you can use it as a dipping sauce for grilled meats or spring rolls or pour over your favorite salad greens.

Serving Size: Makes about 1/2 cup

Cooking Time: 5 minutes

Garlic Lime Dressing

Ingredients:

- 1/4 cup olive oil
- 2 tablespoons lime juice
- 1 clove garlic, minced
- 1 teaspoon honey
- Salt and pepper to taste

Instructions:

1.   Combine olive oil, lime juice, minced garlic, honey, salt, and pepper in the electric wok.

2.   Stir constantly over low heat until the ingredients are well combined.

3.   Allow the dressing to cool down before serving.

4.   Drizzle over salad greens or grilled vegetables when ready to serve.

Serving Size: Makes about 1/4 cup

Cooking Time: 5 minutes

Teriyaki Sauce

Ingredients:

- 1/2 cup soy sauce
- 1/4 cup water
- 2 tablespoons brown sugar
- 1 tablespoon honey
- 2 cloves garlic, minced
- 1 teaspoon grated ginger
- 1 tablespoon cornstarch
- 2 tablespoons water (for cornstarch slurry)

Instructions:

1.   Combine soy sauce, water, brown sugar, honey, minced garlic, and grated ginger in the electric wok.

2.   Next, warm the mixture over medium heat until it starts to simmer.

3.   Create a slurry by mixing/combining cornstarch with water in a small bowl.

4.   Next, pour in the cornstarch slurry into the sauce and cook while stirring constantly until it thickens.

5.   Allow the sauce to cool before serving.

6.   It can be used as a marinade for meats or as a sauce for stir-fries.

Serving Size: Makes about 1 cup

Cooking Time: 10 minutes

Lemon Tahini Dressing

Ingredients:

- 1/4 cup tahini
- 2 tablespoons lemon juice
- 1 tablespoon olive oil
- 1 clove garlic, minced
- 1/4 teaspoon salt
- 2 tablespoons water (optional for thinning)

Instructions:

1. Combine tahini, lemon juice, olive oil, minced garlic, and salt in the electric wok.
2. Stir constantly over low heat until the ingredients are well combined.
3. If the dressing is too thick, add water to reach the desired consistency.
4. Allow the dressing to cool before using.
5. Use the dressing for salads or as a dipping sauce for falafel or grilled vegetables.

Serving Size: Makes about 1/2 cup

Cooking Time: 5 minutes

Ginger Soy Dressing

Ingredients:

- 1/4 cup soy sauce
- 2 tablespoons rice vinegar
- 1 tablespoon honey
- 1 teaspoon grated ginger
- 1 clove garlic, minced
- 1/4 cup olive oil

Instructions:

1. Combine soy sauce, rice vinegar, honey, grated ginger, and minced garlic in the electric wok.

2. Stir constantly and heat over low heat until well combined.

3. Whisk in olive oil until emulsified, then remove from heat.

4. Let the dressing cool down before serving.

5. Use as a marinade for grilled meats or tofu, or serve over salads.

Serving Size: Makes about 1/2 cup

Cooking Time: 5 minutes

Bonus: 21-Day Meal Plan

Week 1:

Day 1:

Breakfast: Vegetable & Tofu Scramble

Lunch: Thai Coconut Soup

Dinner: Teriyaki Chicken Stir-Fry alongside Steamed Rice

Day 2:

Breakfast: Green Onion Pancakes

Lunch: Lentil & Vegetable Soup

Dinner: Beef & Broccoli Stir-Fry with Noodles

Day 3:

Breakfast: Chinese Egg Foo Young

Lunch: Hot & Sour Soup

Dinner: Sweet & Sour Pork with Fried Rice

Day 4:

Breakfast: Banana Pancakes with Honey

Lunch: Miso Soup

Dinner: Shrimp Pad Thai

Day 5:

Breakfast: Veggie Omelette

Lunch: Corn and Potato Chowder

Dinner: Lemon Ginger Salmon with Stir-Fried Vegetables

Day 6:

Breakfast: Breakfast Fried Rice

Lunch: Spicy Peanut Noodles

Dinner: Chicken Curry with Coconut Rice

Day 7:

Breakfast: Berry Smoothie Bowl

Lunch: Tom Yum Soup

Dinner: Vegetable Lo Mein

Week 2:

Day 8:

Breakfast: Avocado Toast with Poached Eggs

Lunch: Szechuan Chicken Salad

Dinner: Sesame Ginger Tofu Stir-Fry with Quinoa

Day 9:

Breakfast: Blueberry Muffins

Lunch: Thai Peanut Noodle Salad

Dinner: Beef and Mushroom Stir-Fry with Jasmine Rice

Day 10:

Breakfast: Greek Yogurt Parfait with Granola

Lunch: Garlic Lime Shrimp Skewers

Dinner: Vegetable Fried Rice with Tofu

Day 11:

Breakfast: Spinach and Feta Frittata

Lunch: Chicken and Vegetable Udon Soup

Dinner: Honey Garlic Glazed Pork Chops with Stir-Fried Bok Choy

Day 12:

Breakfast: Breakfast Burritos

Lunch: Thai Beef Salad

Dinner: Orange Ginger Chicken Stir-Fry with Brown Rice

Day 13:

Breakfast: Apple Cinnamon Oatmeal

Lunch: Sesame Noodle Salad

Dinner: Vegetable Curry with Naan Bread

Day 14:

Breakfast: Peanut Butter Banana Smoothie

Lunch: Vietnamese Pho

Dinner: General Tso's Tofu with Vegetable Chow Mein

Week 3:

Day 15:

Breakfast: Chia Seed Pudding with Fresh Fruit

Lunch: Asian Cucumber Salad

Dinner: Mongolian Beef with Rice Noodles

Day 16:

Breakfast: Quinoa Breakfast Bowl with Berries

Lunch: Egg Drop Soup

Dinner: Chicken and Broccoli Stir-Fry with Udon Noodles

Day 17:

Breakfast: Breakfast Quesadillas with Salsa

Lunch: Thai Green Papaya Salad

Dinner: Sweet Chili Shrimp with Jasmine Rice

Day 18:

Breakfast: Overnight Oats with Almond Butter

Lunch: Korean Kimchi Soup

Dinner: Beef and Bell Pepper Stir-Fry with Vermicelli Noodles

Day 19:

Breakfast: Spinach and Mushroom Breakfast Burritos

Lunch: Thai Cucumber Salad

Dinner: Teriyaki Salmon with Stir-Fried Zucchini

Day 20:

Breakfast: Coconut Chia Pudding with Mango

Lunch: Vietnamese Spring Rolls with Peanut Dipping Sauce

Dinner: Tofu & Vegetable Stir-Fry with Brown Rice

Day 21:

Breakfast: Breakfast Smoothie with Spinach and Pineapple

Lunch: Chinese Chicken Salad

Dinner: Sesame Crusted Tuna with Asian Slaw

Conclusion

You've successfully completed our Electric Wok Cookbook for Beginners. We trust this culinary journey has motivated you to explore the adaptability and convenience of using an electric wok for cooking. From sizzling stir-fries to flavorful soups and mouthwatering sauces, this cookbook has exposed you to a variety of delightful possibilities.

By mastering the fundamental techniques and experimenting with a range of recipes, you've initiated your journey toward becoming a self-assured home chef. Whether you're preparing meals for yourself or your family or hosting guests, the electric wok provides limitless opportunities to effortlessly create quick and tasty dishes.

As you progress in your culinary explorations, feel free to try out various ingredients, flavors, and cooking techniques. Let your imagination come alive and personalize each dish. And bear in mind cooking is not just about fueling the body but also nourishing the soul. Embrace the process, relish every mouthful, and spread the joy of good food with those around you.

We appreciate you selecting our cookbook to join you on this adventure. We trust it has given you valuable knowledge, helpful suggestions, and, most importantly, delectable recipes to relish for years to come.

We are deeply thankful to all our readers for their support and excitement throughout the development of this cookbook. Your curiosity in discovering the world of electric wok cooking has been our motivation, and we are privileged to have embarked on this culinary journey with you.

We also want to show our gratitude to the chefs, food aficionados, and culinary professionals whose knowledge and love have influenced the recipes showcased in this book. Your commitment to the art of cooking has enhanced our culinary world and provided limitless inspiration for home cooks everywhere.

Finally, we express our gratitude to our friends and family for their constant support and motivation during this journey. Your support and inspiration have sparked our creativity and driven us to bring this cookbook to fruition.

As you start exploring the world of cooking with your electric wok, we hope you have enjoyable culinary experiences and create lasting memories. May each dish become a tribute to great food, wonderful company, and the pleasure of sharing delightful flavors with your loved ones.

Made in the USA
Columbia, SC
05 February 2025

53307907R00054